ANIMALS
That Make a Difference!

Lynx

Ashley Lee

Explore other books at:
WWW.ENGAGEBOOKS.COM

VANCOUVER, B.C.

ℯ➚ WWW.ENGAGEBOOKS.COM

Lynx: Pre-1
Animals That Make a Difference!
Lee, Ashley, 1995
Text © 2025 Engage Books
Design © 2025 Engage Books

Edited by: A.R. Roumanis, and Ashley Lee
Design by: Mandy Christiansen

Text set in Arial Regular.

FIRST EDITION / FIRST PRINTING

library and archives canada cataloguing in publication

Title: Lynx / Ashley Lee.
Names: Lee, Ashley, author.
Description: Series statement: Animals that make a difference

Identifiers: Canadiana (print) 20230448542 | Canadiana (ebook) 20230448569
ISBN 978-1-77878-691-4 (hardcover)
ISBN 978-1-77878-700-3 (softcover)

Subjects:
LCSH: Lynx—Juvenile literature.
LCSH: Human-animal relationships—Juvenile literature.

Classification: LCC QL737.P94 C38 2025 | DDC J599.885—DC23

This project has been made possible in part
by the Government of Canada.

Canada

Careful! Lynx are not as cuddly as they look!

Lynx are a kind of cat.

Their yellow eyes
glow in the dark.

Lynx have short tails.

The end is always black.

Lynx have long black fur on the tops of their ears.

Some lynx have really big feet.

The bottoms are covered in fur.

11

Big, furry feet help
lynx walk in the snow.

Lynx eat small animals.

They will eat birds, rabbits, and beavers.

Lynx eat animals that make babies quickly.

Too many animals in one place eat all the food.

Eating these animals helps make sure other animals have food.

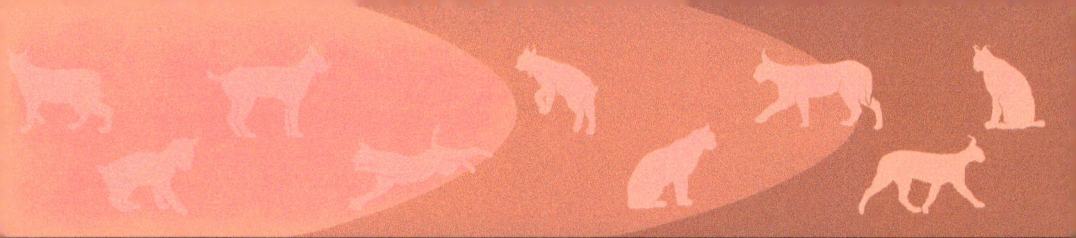

19

Lynx live in Europe, Asia, and North America.

They often
live in forests.

Lynx often live alone in dens.

A den is a kind of hidden hole.

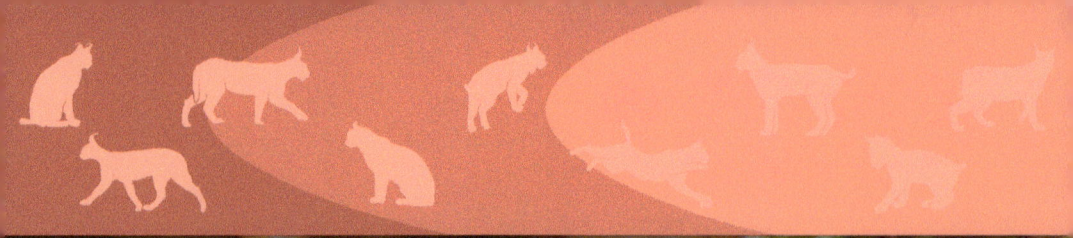

Lynx have one to four babies.

They are born
in the spring.

Lynx leave their moms after about a year.

They live for
10 to 15 years.

27

Many lynx
are in danger.

People are hunting them and cutting down their forests.

Quiz

Test your knowledge of lynx by answering the following questions. The questions are based on what you have read in this book. The answers are listed on the bottom of the next page.

1 Are lynx a kind of cat?

2 Do lynx have short tails?

3 Do big, furry feet help lynx walk in the snow?

4 Do Lynx often live in forests?

5 Are lynx babies born in the spring?

6 Are many lynx in danger?

Explore other books in the
Animals That Make a Difference series

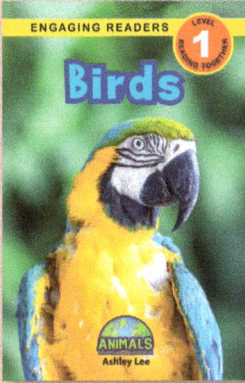

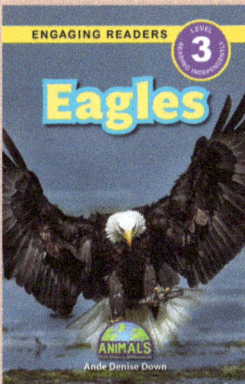

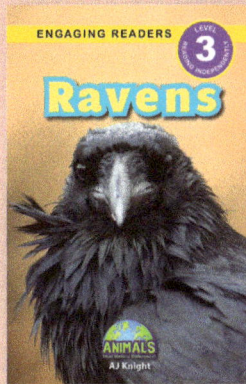

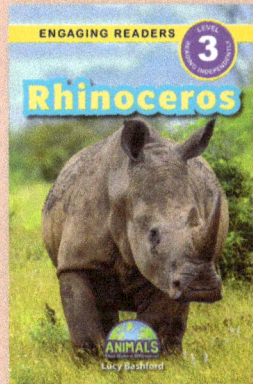

ENGAGING READERS — LEVEL 1 — READING TOGETHER
Birds
ANIMALS
Ashley Lee

ENGAGING READERS — LEVEL 1 — READING TOGETHER
Ladybugs
ANIMALS
Ashley Lee

ENGAGING READERS — LEVEL 1 — READING TOGETHER
Squirrels
ANIMALS
Ashley Lee

ENGAGING READERS — LEVEL 2 — READING WITH HELP
Butterflies
ANIMALS
Ashley Lee

ENGAGING READERS — LEVEL 2 — READING WITH HELP
Frogs
ANIMALS
Ashley Lee

ENGAGING READERS — LEVEL 2 — READING WITH HELP
Octopuses
ANIMALS
Ashley Lee

ENGAGING READERS — LEVEL 3 — READING INDEPENDENTLY
Eagles
ANIMALS
Ande Denise Down

ENGAGING READERS — LEVEL 3 — READING INDEPENDENTLY
Ravens
ANIMALS
AJ Knight

ENGAGING READERS — LEVEL 3 — READING INDEPENDENTLY
Rhinoceros
ANIMALS
Lucy Bashford

Visit www.engagebooks.com to explore more Engaging Readers.

www.ingramcontent.com/pod-product-compliance
Lightning Source LLC
Chambersburg PA
CBHW052036030426
42337CB00027B/5025